T0332510

A Short Guide to
Consumer Rights in Construction Contracts

Roland Phillips

RIBA ⑅ **Publishing**

© RIBA Enterprises Ltd., 2010

Published by RIBA Publishing, 15 Bonhill Street, London EC2P 2EA

ISBN 978 1 85946 384 0

Stock code 73704

The right of Roland Phillips to be identified as the Author of this Work has been asserted in accordance with the Copyright, Design and Patents Act 1988

British Library Cataloguing in Publications Data
A catalogue record for this book is available from the British Library.

Publisher: Steven Cross
Commissioning Editor: James Thompson
Project Editor: Gray Publishing
Designed and typeset by Gray Publishing, Tunbridge Wells
Printed and bound by Windsor Print, Tonbridge

While every effort has been made to check the accuracy and quality of the information given in this publication, neither the Author nor the Publisher accept any responsibility for the subsequent use of this information, for any errors or omissions that it may contain, or for any misunderstandings arising from it. All parties must rely exclusively upon their own skill and judgement or upon their advisers when using this publication and RIBA Enterprises Ltd. assumes no liability to any user or any third party.

RIBA Publishing is part of RIBA Enterprises Ltd.
www.ribaenterprises.com

Cover photo: © Ant Clausen

Contents

About the author

Roland Phillips RIBA commenced his professional life with Tecton in 1948; subsequently becoming a partner in private practice, until joining the National Health Service, practising as a regional architect and finally as managing director of the project management division of a PLC.

He has served on the RIBA Contracts Committee, the RIBA Appointments Group, the Joint Contracts Tribunal and is editor of the *RIBA Agreements*.

1 Introduction

1.1 Who is this guide for?

This guide is for all professional advisors and contractors who advise on or make a contract with a consumer.

1.2 Who is a consumer?

In UK legislation, a 'consumer' means a natural person who is acting for purposes outside his or her business, that is a person who completes a contract in his or her own name, not as a limited company or other legal entity.

In certain circumstances, a company may also be a 'consumer', subject to Unfair Contract Terms Act 1977 (but not The Unfair Terms in Consumer Contracts Regulations 1999) if the transaction is only incidental to its business activity and which is not of a kind it makes with any degree of regularity. Although not obligatory, it may be a wise precaution and courteous to treat such companies as though The Unfair Terms in Consumer Contracts Regulations 1999 did apply.

1.3 Why is this guide needed?

The legislation is designed to protect consumers, and as a result professional advisors and contractors have some significant obligations in the process of reaching and making a contract with a consumer.

This guide outlines the scope of the relevant legislation and its effect on the terms of professional services agreements and/or building contracts. The guide cannot replace careful study of the legislation.

There are a number of people who have discovered the unhappy consequences of failing to comply with the statutory arrangements.

1.4 What is the legislation?

The key statutes are:

- The Provision of Services Regulations SI 2009/2999

- Unfair Contract Terms Act 1977

- The Unfair Terms in Consumer Contracts Regulations SI 1999/2083 (UTCCR)

- The Cancellation of Contracts made in a Consumer's Home or Place of Work etc. Regulations SI 2008/1816.

Acts of Parliament are available at www.opsi.gov.uk/acts and Statutory Instruments (Regulations) are available at www.opsi. gov.uk/stat.

1.4.1 Exemption from other legislation

For work to a consumer's home, including a new home, a consumer will be exempt from any statutory duties arising from:

a. Housing Grants, Construction and Regeneration Act 1996 (as amended) (HGCRA) as a 'residential occupier'

b. The Construction (Design and Management) Regulations SI 2007/320 (CDM Regulations)

c. The Late Payment of Commercial Debts (Interest) Regulations SI 2002/1674.

Exemptions (a) and (b) will not apply:

- if the contract relates to a consumer's second home which is to be let at any time as a holiday rental or to other tenants

- if the consumer is not a 'residential occupier' or a 'domestic client' as defined in the CDM Regulations.

If the client is a married couple or joint residential occupiers, for example, all the client parties are consumers, but one of their number could be chosen as their representative with full authority to act on behalf of the parties and to sign the contract.

2 The Provision of Services Regulations SI 2009/2999

2.1 Introduction

These Regulations require 'service providers' (for example, professional advisors and building contractors) to make available to 'service recipients'[1] (for example, clients and potential clients) information about the provider's business and the handling of complaints.

A guide to the Regulations is available at www.berr.gov.uk/files/file53100.pdf.

'Made available' means (Regulation 8.2) that the required information:

a. is supplied by the provider to the recipient on the provider's own initiative

b. is easily accessible to the recipient at the place where the service is provided or the contract for the service is concluded

c. is easily accessible to the recipient electronically by means of an address supplied by the provider, or

---

1   The Regulations also apply to 'service recipients' other than consumers.

d. appears in any information document supplied to the recipient by the provider in which the provider gives a detailed description of the service.

The required information is to be 'made available' in a clear and unambiguous manner in good time before the conclusion of a written contract, or where no written contract is yet in place, before the services are provided.

2.2   What information needs to be supplied?

The information required by the Regulations is about the provider's business and is not project specific. It is to include the legal status of the business, contact details of its professional insurance supplier and its complaints procedure, together with details of websites of relevant regulating bodies relating to codes of conduct and the availability of any non-judicial dispute resolution procedures.

The Regulations apply to any business providing services and its principals, but not to employees. However, the information might include generic data about personnel with specialist qualifications relevant to the performance of the business, for example, the number of accredited conservation architects or approved inspectors.

If the business is registered in another state within the European Economic Area, the information should include particulars of the relevant authority or the point of single contact in that state.

2.2.1 Professional advisors

Principals, who are members of a professional institution, should be identified in the information giving the name of the institution and their registration number.

The term 'regulated profession' in the Regulations applies to a professional activity or group of activities:

- where possession of specified qualifications is required by legislation, or

- where use of a professional title is limited to holders of a given professional qualification.

The first category applies to architects and approved inspectors. Architects are regulated by the Architects Registration Board under the Architects Act 1997 and approved inspectors are regulated by the Construction Industry Council under the Building Act 1984 as amended.

The second category applies to other professionals who are regulated by the relevant professional institution(s) with which they are registered. Members of the Royal Institute of British Architects and the Association of Consultant Approved Inspectors are also regulated by those bodies.

If the business is regulated by a professional body for its members, such as the APS Register of Practices, the Landscape Institute Registered Practices, the RIBA Chartered Practices and RICS Regulated Practices, this should be noted in the information.

It should not be necessary to repeat in the information the project-specific data about the applicable law, liability, fees and methods of calculation, expenses, professional liability insurance, dispute resolution and the services, which will be found in all 'standard' professional services agreements.

2.2.2 Contractors

Contractors should include details of membership of a trade association, registration in a trade or other similar public register, contact details of their professional liability insurer and the territorial coverage, any applicable codes of conduct and the websites from which these codes are available.

In addition to the preliminary checks on potential contractors (for example, on financial status, quality, health and safety systems, relevant experience, etc.), the architect/contract administrator or other consultant should also ascertain that the required information is available before inviting tenders.

Some of the information required by the Regulations will be provided in the completed building contract, for example, applicable law, liability, payments and method of calculation, expenses, professional liability insurance (if applicable) and the services to be provided.

3 The Unfair Terms in Consumer Contracts Regulations SI 1999/2083

3.1 Introduction

These Regulations are to protect consumers from inappropriate provisions imposed by a supplier.

Regulation 5(1) says: 'a contractual term which has not been **individually negotiated** shall be regarded as unfair if, contrary to the requirement of good faith, it causes a significant imbalance in the parties' rights and obligations under the contract to the detriment of the consumer'.

Regulation 5(2) says: 'a term shall always be regarded as not having been individually negotiated where it has been drafted in advance and the consumer has therefore not been able to influence the substance of the term'.

Regulation 5(4) says: 'it shall be for any seller or supplier who claims that a term was individually negotiated to show that it was'.

Schedule 2 (indicative and non-exhaustive list of terms which may be regarded as unfair) includes terms that are of particular relevance to construction contracts:

- 1(b) refers to 'inappropriately excluding or limiting the legal rights of the consumer *vis-à-vis* the seller or supplier in the event of total or partial non-performance or inadequate performance by the seller supplier or of any of the contractual obligations, including the option of offsetting a debt owed to the seller or supplier against any claim'

- 1(i) refers to 'irrevocably binding the consumer to terms with which he had no real opportunity of becoming acquainted before the conclusion of the contract'

- 1(q) refers to 'excluding or hindering the consumer's right to take legal action or exercise any other legal remedy, particularly by requiring the consumer to take disputes exclusively to arbitration not covered by legal provisions ...'.

3.2 Negotiating the terms of a contract

The terms of a contract should be read through with the consumer and each term individually negotiated in the context of UTCCR. The aim of the negotiations should be to minimise the risk that subsequently any term could be considered to be unfair. It is not unheard of for a consumer to claim, when things go wrong, that he or she did not understand the implications of a term.

A professional advisor or contractor should not proceed with the provision of goods or services if there is any uncertainty about the terms of the contract, unless instructed to do so and the instructions are confirmed in writing. This could be very important if the consumer decides to cancel the agreement (see section 4).

If amendment to, or deletion of, the provisions are required, carefully consider the impact on other provisions and any change to liabilities. The substance of the negotiations should be recorded and attached to the contract to show that it accords with the Regulations.

There are some notable differences between generic contracts for professional services and for building works. Both will comply with, or provide, contractual alternatives to statutory requirements, but the negotiations or explanations should cover those requirements that do not (or need not) apply to 'residential occupiers' or consumers (see section 1.4.1).

Failure to explain the consequences of using unamended standard contracts might make a professional advisor liable to the consumer client for damages or a contractor might lose the protection of the contract in a dispute.

A professional services contract may specify contractual limitation of the period of and amount of liability. A building contract does not. In relation to time, the Limitation Act 1980 and the Latent Damage Act 1986 will apply, except in the JCT home owner/occupier forms of contract, suitable for simple works, that specify 'for 6 years after carrying out the work the builder will remain responsible for any faults in the work (other than fair wear and tear) which are caused by him'.

A professional services contract may cover copyright, professional indemnity insurance and exclude the right of set-off and the operation of joint and several liability, as in a net contribution clause.

Building contracts usually require the contractor to insure against claims arising from damage to property, other than the works, and loss or damage to the works caused by specified perils. In the case of existing buildings, this insurance may be taken out by the client. In the case of a contractor's design, the contractor may be required to provide professional indemnity insurance.

3.2.1 Disputes

A consumer has the right to refer any dispute to the courts. Any other options must be negotiated. For instance, the consumer could opt to retain the provisions for arbitration, perhaps to keep the matter private. Or, if a consumer chooses adjudication, the RIBA[2] or RICS Adjudication Scheme for Consumer Contracts, which may be suitable for low-value claims, could be selected, perhaps in addition to, and as an alternative to, the procedures published by the Construction Industry Council or the relevant Scheme for Construction Contracts Regulations 1998.

If it cannot be demonstrated that the contract terms were agreed, there will be no provision for adjudication or arbitration and disputes will be settled in court.

3.3 Negotiating the terms of a professional services contract

While the RIBA Conditions of Appointment and other similar forms provide remedies for the client in the event of default by the professional advisor, for example, the requirement to maintain professional indemnity insurance and the options for dispute resolution, all of the terms need careful explanation in the negotiations.

---

2 Details of the RIBA scheme are available from RIBA's Disputes Resolution Office.

3.4 Negotiating the terms of a building contract

The architect/contract administrator or other consultant providing pre-construction services has a duty to advise a consumer client on the powers and duties of the parties under the building contract and, in particular, the contractual provisions arising from or in place of, the relevant legislation. The advice should be given at the time the tender documents and the terms of the contract are being prepared.

The contractor must negotiate the terms of the building contract, unless it is confirmed that the employer has been properly advised.

3.5 Case law

In *Westminster Building Company* v. *Andrew Beckingham* [2004] EWHC 138 (TCC) the claimant contractor was successful in appealing against an adjudicator's award because the provision for adjudication had not been individually negotiated. The court noted that the client had competent and objective advice from his professional advisor. Similarly in *Bryan and Langley Limited* v. *Boston* the court found in favour of the contractor and noted that the JCT building contract had been imposed by the consumer, through his surveyor.

In *Domsalla* v. *Dyason* EWHC 1174 (TCC) the builder, who sued for non-payment of an interim valuation because no withholding notice had been issued, lost because the builder was unaware that the terms of a contract with a consumer had to be negotiated.

It is not recorded whether any advisors to those consumer clients were pursued for negligence.

In *Picardi* v. *Cuniberti* [2002] EWHC 2923 (TCC) the architect sought to enforce an adjudicator's award based on unsigned documents. The court found that the contract terms were never agreed, there was no adjudication provision and the adjudication was therefore invalid, that is, the client was not bound to pay the disputed invoices.

4 The right to cancel a contract

4.1 Introduction

The Cancellation of Contracts made in a Consumer's Home or Place of Work etc. Regulations SI 2008/1816 establishes the right of a consumer to cancel a contract within seven days from the date when it is made during a visit by a trader to the consumer's home or place of work or on an excursion organised by the trader or an unsolicited visit by the trader when the contract relates to:[3]

a. the construction of extensions, patios, conservatories or driveways

b. the supply of goods and their incorporation in immovable property

c. the repair, refurbishment or improvement of immovable property.

The Regulations do not apply to a contract for the construction, sale or rental of immovable property or to an agreement provided that each of the following conditions is met:[4]

---

3   SI 2008/1816: Schedule 3, paragraph 3.1.
4   SI 2008/1816: Schedule 3, paragraph 3.3.

d. the contract is concluded on the basis of a contract which the consumer has a proper opportunity of reading in the absence of the trader's representative

e. there is intended to be continuity of contact between trader's representative and the consumer in relation to that or any subsequent transaction

f. the contract contains a prominent notice informing the consumer of his or her right to cancel the contract within the period of seven days after the consumer signed the contract.

Unless such a provision is included in the contract there are two options:

■ A. Amend the contract to include a relevant clause before it is presented for signature. The draft clause (see pages 22 and 23) will comply with condition (f) above and conditions (d) and (e) will be met by the negotiation process necessary to avoid conflict with the UTCCR (see section 3).

The draft clause covers any place where the contract will be made (signed) by the consumer and any contract, including construction of a new home. It is less complicated than the Regulations and more relevant to signing a negotiated agreement.

Providing the clause is explained to the client, there will be no need to provide a separate notice of the right to cancel.

■ B. Serve a 'Notice of the right to cancel'[5] (see the draft on pages 24 and 25) on or before the contract is presented for

---

5   A copy of the draft notice can be downloaded free of charge from: www.ribabookshops.com/letter-contracts.

signature. The notice may be sent by post or by email or given in person.

It is important to note that the right operates from the date when the contract is made or, if later, the day when the notice is received by the consumer.

For instance, if work commences, whether or not an instruction was given in writing by the client, in all probability a contract is made and the professional advisor or contractor is under an obligation to notify the client of the right to cancel within seven days from the day the notice is served.

If no notice is given before the contract is made, the consumer's right to cancel is not extinguished and could be activated by the issue of a cancellation notice at any time.

Failure to give a notice is liable on summary conviction to a fine of up to £5000.

For obvious reasons, the professional advisor or contractor should use every endeavour to get the contract signed before starting work and investing time and energy in case the consumer has second thoughts, even though the Regulations provide for protection of costs due for work up to the end of the seven-day period.

But note that confirmation in writing by the client or professional advisor or contractor of any instruction to proceed is a prerequisite for payment for any goods or services provided before a cancellation notice is received.

4.2 Cancelling a professional services agreement

The consumer client should be advised of the right to cancel when the terms of the agreement are negotiated by the professional advisor (see section 3).

Unless the agreement already provides for the right to cancel, it is recommended that option A (the inclusion of a draft clause see page 22) is implemented, obviating the need for a separate notice. If this is not done and the agreement is sent to the client for signature by the professional advisor, then option B, the notice of the right to cancel should be given at the same time.

> The following draft clause and notice can be downloaded free of charge from www.ribabookshops.com/consumerrights

4.2.1 Option A – draft clause Appendix number <reference>

Consumer's right to cancel:[6,7]

1 The Client has the right to cancel this agreement for any reason by delivering or sending (including by electronic mail) a cancellation notice to <the professional advisor> at any time within the period of 7 days starting from the date when the Client signed this agreement.

2 The notice of cancellation is deemed to be served as soon as it is posted or sent to <the professional advisor> or in the case of an electronic communication from the day it is sent to <the professional advisor>.

3 <the professional advisor> shall be entitled to any fees and expenses properly due before <the professional advisor> receives the notice of cancellation, if before the end of the 7 day period <the professional advisor> was instructed to perform any services and the instruction or instructions were confirmed in writing.

4 The notice is to be addressed to <the professional advisor> and state:

---

6   This clause is to be boxed as shown to comply with the Regulations.
7   Text between <symbols> indicates information to be entered by the sender. Text in [square brackets] should be project specific or may be deleted.

<Name of client> hereby gives notice that the agreement with <the professional advisor> <insert name> and signed [on our behalf] by <name of person(s) who signed> on <date of signing> is cancelled.

<Client signature(s)>

<address>

<date>

Whether the clause is inserted into the contract electronically or in a separate amendment, it should be initialled by the parties.

4.2.2 Option B. Draft notice of right to cancel a professional services agreement

From <professional advisor's business address>

To <consumer's name and address>

For the attention of <the person or persons who will sign on behalf of the consumer>

Dear [Mr] [and] [Mrs] [<name>] [Sir] [Madam]

[Project] [at] [reference]

Notice of the right to cancel[8]

The Cancellation of Contracts made in a Consumer's Home or Place of Work etc. Regulations 2008

These Regulations establish your right to cancel the agreement for this project, within the period of 7 days starting with the date on which you sign the contract or if later the day of receipt of this notice.

If you wish to cancel the agreement, you must do so in writing by serving a cancellation notice in the form described below.

The notice will be deemed to have been served as soon as it is given in person, posted or sent by electronic communication.

8   Text between <symbols> indicates information to be entered by the sender. Text in [square brackets] should be project specific or may be deleted.

If you cancel this agreement you may have to pay any fees and expenses properly due before the notice of cancellation is received, if you instructed performance of any services and the instruction or instructions were confirmed in writing before you signed the agreement or before the end of the 7 day period.

<professional advisor's signature>

For and on behalf of <company name>

The notice is to be addressed to <the name of professional advisor> at:

<postal address or electronic mail address>

For the attention of <M ...>

and state:

<Name of client> hereby gives notice that the agreement with <name of professional advisor> and signed [on our behalf] by <name of person(s) who signed> on <date of signing> is cancelled.

<Client's signature(s)>

<address>

4.3   Cancelling a building contract

The consumer should be advised of the right to cancel when the terms of the contract are explained by a professional advisor or negotiated by the contractor – see section 3.

As most published building contracts do not allow for the right to cancel, other than contracts specifically for consumers, for example, the JCT Building contract for a homeowner/occupier, it is recommended that option A is implemented, obviating the need for a separate notice.

If this is not done and the contract is sent to the client for signature by the architect/contract administrator, the notice of the right to cancel should be given at the same time by the sender and copied to the contractor.

If the contract is sent by the contractor, the notice is given by the contractor.

The following draft clause and notice can be downloaded free of charge from www.ribabookshops.com/consumerrights

4.3.1 Option A. Draft clause Appendix number <reference>

Consumer's right to cancel:[9,10]

1 The Employer has the right to cancel this contract for any reason by delivering or sending (including by electronic mail) a cancellation notice to the Contractor at any time within the period of 7 days starting from the date when the Employer signed this Agreement.

2 The notice of cancellation is deemed to be served as soon as it is posted or sent to the Contractor or in the case of an electronic communication from the day it is sent to the Contractor.

3 If the Employer cancels this Agreement:

- the Contractor shall be entitled to payment for any goods supplied or purchased by the Contractor for the Project and any work carried out before the Contractor receives the notice of cancellation, if before the end of the 7 day period, the Contractor was instructed to provide any goods or services and the instruction or instructions were confirmed in writing; or

---

9 This clause is to be boxed as shown to comply with the Regulations.

10 Text between <symbols> indicates information to be entered by the sender. Text in [square brackets] should be project specific or may be deleted.

- the Contractor will refund any money the Employer paid in connection with this contract

4 The notice is to be addressed to the Contractor and state:

<Name of Employer> hereby gives notice that the contract with the <name of Contractor> and signed [on our behalf] by <name of person(s) who signed> on <date of signing> is cancelled.

<Employer signature(s)>

<address>

<date>

Whether the clause is inserted into the contract electronically or in a separate amendment, it should be initialled by the parties.

4.3.2 Option B. Draft notice of right to cancel a building contract [11]

From <sender's business address>

To <consumer's name and address>

For the attention of <the person or persons who will sign on behalf of the consumer>

Dear [Mr] [and] [Mrs] [<name>] [Sir] [Madam]

[Project] [at] [reference]

Notice of the right to cancel[6]

The Cancellation of Contracts made in a Consumer's Home or Place of Work etc. Regulations 2008

These Regulations establish your right to cancel the contract for this project, within the period of 7 days starting with the date on which you sign the contract or if later the day of receipt of this notice.

If you wish to cancel the contract, you must do so in writing by serving a cancellation notice in the form described below.

The notice will be deemed to have been served as soon as it is given in person, posted or sent by electronic communication.

11 Text between <symbols> indicates information to be entered by the sender. Text in [square brackets] should be project specific or may be deleted.

If you cancel this contract:

the contractor will refund any money you paid in connection with this contract; or

you may have to pay for any goods or services provided before the notice of cancellation is received, if you instructed the provision of any goods or services in writing before you signed the contract or before the end of the 7 day period.

<Sender's signature>

For and on behalf of <company name>

Copy to [contractor] [architect/contract administrator]

The notice is to be addressed to the contractor at:

<postal address or electronic mail address>

For the attention of <M ...>

and state:

<Name of Employer> hereby gives notice that the contract with the <name of contractor> and signed [on our behalf] by <name of person(s) who signed> on <date of signing> is cancelled.

<Employer's signature(s)>

<address>

<date>

NB: A copy the cancellation notice should be sent to the architect/contract administrator, if applicable.

Further reading

RIBA Agreements 2010

Electronic RIBA Agreements are available to purchase at:
www.ribabookshops/agreements

Agreements also available in print:

RIBA Standard Agreement 2010 – Architect
RIBA Standard Agreement 2010 – Consultant
RIBA Concise Agreement 2010 – Architect
RIBA Concise Agreement 2010 – Consultant
RIBA Domestic Project Agreement 2010 – Architect
RIBA Domestic Project Agreement 2010 – Consultant
RIBA Sub-consultant Agreement 2010

Other publications

Phillips, R., *A client's guide to engaging an architect*, November 2009 Revision (RIBA Publishing, 2009).

Phillips, R., *A guide to letter contracts: for very small projects surveys and reports*, Second edition, (RIBA Publishing, 2010).

Phillips, R., *Guide to RIBA Agreements 2010* (RIBA Publishing, 2010).

RIBA, *RIBA Agreements 2010: Electronic-only components* (RIBA Publishing, 2010).